Viola Time Run

Piano accompaniment book

Kathy and David Blackwell

Teacher's note

These piano parts are written to accompany the tunes in *Viola Time Runners*. They are an alternative to the viola duet accompaniments or CD, and are not designed to be used with those items. A separate violin piano accompaniment book is available providing parts for when violas play together with violins using *Fiddle Time Runners*.

Kathy and David Blackwell

MUSIC DEPARTMENT

OXFORD
UNIVERSITY PRESS

UNIVERSITY PRESS

Great Clarendon Street, Oxford OX2 6DP,
United Kingdom

Oxford University Press is a department of the University of Oxford.
It furthers the University's objective of excellence in research, scholarship,
and education by publishing worldwide. Oxford is a registered trade mark of
Oxford University Press in the UK and in certain other countries

ISBN 978-0-19-339853-5

Cover illustration by Martin Remphry

Music and text origination by Katie Johnston
Printed in Great Britain on acid-free paper by
Halstan & Co. Ltd, Amersham, Bucks.

Contents

1. Start the show

KB & DB

Rock tempo

2. Banyan tree

C string special

Jamaican

3. Heat haze

KB & DB

4. Medieval tale

KB & DB

5. In memory

for Eileen

C string special

KB & DB

6. Chase in the dark

KB & DB

With menace

7. Merrily danced the Quaker's wife

Scottish

8. *O leave your sheep:* page 14

9. Jingle bells

J. Pierpont

Nos. 8 and 9 are reversed to avoid a page turn.

14

8. O leave your sheep

C string special

Traditional

10. Allegretto in C

Mozart

11. Pick a bale of cotton

American

12. Noël

C string special

Daquin

13. Finale from the 'Water Music'

Handel

14. Ecossaise in G

Beethoven

15. Viola Time rag

KB & DB

Not too fast

16. Playing on the ol' banjo

17. On the go!

KB & DB

* The repeat is written out in full in the viola part.

18. Blue whale: page 26

19. Takin' it easy

KB & DB

Laid-back tempo

2nd time **to Coda**

* The repeat is written out in full in the viola part.
Nos. 18 and 19 are reversed to avoid a page turn.

18. Blue whale

C string special

KB & DB

20. Mean street chase

C string special

KB & DB

Funky

21. Ten thousand miles away

C string special

Sea shanty

22. I got those viola blues

KB & DB

23. Air in C

J. C. Bach

24. Prelude from 'Te Deum'

Charpentier

25. That's how it goes!

KB & DB

26. Flamenco dance

KB & DB

27. Somebody's knocking at your door

Traditional

28. The old chariot

Sea shanty

29. Adam in the garden

Jamaican

42 30. Air: page 44

31. The wee cooper o' Fife

Scottish

Gently

Nos. 30 and 31 are reversed to avoid a page turn.

30. Air

Handel

32. Aerobics!

KB & DB

33. Caribbean sunshine

KB & DB

18. Yodelling song

Traditional

This piece is an alternative to No. 18 Blue whale (C string special) and can be found in the Ensemble parts section of the pupil book.

20. Gypsy dance

KB & DB

This piece is an alternative to No. 20 Mean street chase (C string special) and can be found in the Ensemble parts section of the pupil book.